DETECTING DISASTERS

DETECTING
TSUNAMIS

by Marne Ventura

FOCUS
READERS

WWW.NORTHSTAREDITIONS.COM

Produced for North Star Editions by Red Line Editorial.

Photographs ©: Kyodo News/AP Images, cover, 1; Suzanne Plunkett/AP Images, 4–5; Enwaer/Xinhua/AP Images, 6; Eugene Hoshiko/AP Images, 9; Chris Butler/Science Source, 10–11; José Antonio Peñas/Science Source, 13; Marisa Estivill/Shutterstock Images, 14; Science Source, 16–17; Marco Garcia/AP Images, 19; NOAA, 20; Gwen Shockey/Science Source, 23; ChameleonsEye/Shutterstock Images, 24–25; Lars Nicolaysen/picture-alliance/dpa/AP Images, 26

Content Consultant: Gerard Fryer, Senior Geophysicist, NOAA Pacific Tsunami Warning Center

ISBN
978-1-63517-005-4 (hardcover)
978-1-63517-061-0 (paperback)
978-1-63517-167-9 (ebook pdf)
978-1-63517-117-4 (hosted ebook)

Library of Congress Control Number: 2016949752

Printed in the United States of America
Mankato, MN
May, 2018

ABOUT THE AUTHOR

Marne Ventura is the author of 41 books for kids. She loves writing about nature, science, technology, food, health, and crafts. She is a former elementary school teacher and holds a master's degree in education from the University of California. Marne lives with her husband on the central coast of California.

TABLE OF CONTENTS

CHAPTER 1

Tsunami! 5

CHAPTER 2

The Science Behind Tsunamis 11

CHAPTER 3

Tsunami Detection 17

A CLOSER LOOK

Deep-Ocean Assessment and Reporting of Tsunamis (DART) 22

CHAPTER 4

Tsunami Safety 25

Tsunami Safety Checklist • 29
Focus on Detecting Tsunamis • 30
Glossary • 31
To Learn More • 32
Index • 32

TSUNAMI!

Marine biologist Dwayne Meadows was on vacation in Thailand. It was December 26, 2004. Meadows was getting ready to go diving. Suddenly, shouts rang out nearby.

Meadows looked outside. Something was wrong. The ocean was usually a few steps away from his small beach house.

The 2004 tsunami totally destroyed many buildings along the shores of Thailand.

Indonesia was the country hit hardest by the 2004 tsunami.

Now the water was farther from shore. Fish flopped on the wet sand. A wall of murky water with a foamy white top loomed in the distance. Meadows recognized what was happening. It was a tsunami.

He turned to jump out the back window so he could run to higher ground. Suddenly, the wave hit the house and ripped away the front wall. Meadows was underwater. It took him almost a minute to find his way to the surface. At last, his head rose above the water. He gasped for breath.

When the water finally calmed, he looked around. He was a quarter mile (400 m) from shore. The houses along the beach were washed away.

Meadows's knee hurt, and his hands were bleeding. He swam toward shore. When he reached land, he saw another wave coming. He ran for higher ground.

Broken glass, twisted metal, and splintered wood lay all around. He finally reached a resort where people were helping others who had been hurt.

WHAT CAUSED THE INDIAN OCEAN TSUNAMI?

A powerful earthquake that began near the west coast of the Indonesian island of Sumatra caused the 2004 Indian Ocean tsunami. It was the third-strongest earthquake in recorded history. The quake lifted the sea floor by as much as 20 feet (6.1 m). This pushed the ocean up, forming a lump of water. Gravity made the lump collapse, creating the tsunami. The tsunami waves moved across the Indian Ocean as fast as a jet plane.

Volunteer rescue workers from around the world came to the affected areas to help.

The 2004 Indian Ocean tsunami struck Thailand, Indonesia, Sri Lanka, and India. More than 230,000 people were killed. Half a million others were injured. It was the deadliest tsunami in recorded history. By learning how to detect these waves and issue warnings quickly, scientists can save many lives in future tsunamis.

CHAPTER 2

THE SCIENCE BEHIND TSUNAMIS

A tsunami is a series of very long ocean waves. The distance from one **crest** to the next can be as much as 100 miles (160 km). The name *tsunami* comes from the Japanese words *tsu*, meaning "harbor," and *nami*, meaning "waves." Tsunami waves can grow to be as tall as a 10-story building.

Tsunami waves become increasingly dangerous as they approach and strike land.

Far out at sea, these waves do not usually cause damage or death. But when a tsunami strikes land, it can be incredibly destructive. The waves can sweep away everything in their path.

WIND OR A TSUNAMI?

The waves you see on a normal day at the beach are caused by wind moving over the water. The time from one wave to the next is often approximately 10 seconds. Tsunami waves are different. When movement on the ocean floor **displaces** water, it creates waves that can each last 15 to 25 minutes. Together, these long waves make up a tsunami. As wind waves move, they get smaller. Tsunami waves lose their energy more slowly. They grow as they reach the shore.

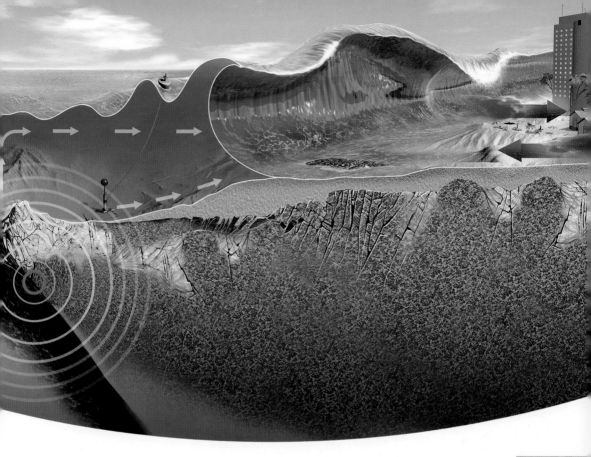

The energy released in an earthquake leads to the displacement of water responsible for tsunamis.

Sometimes tsunamis are called tidal waves, but they do not come from the normal forces that cause tides. Earthquakes are the most common cause of tsunamis. Earth's crust is made up of **plates** that are always moving.

Cities along coastlines and near earthquake-prone areas are at risk from tsunamis.

Sometimes two plates bump into each other and stick. Energy builds up until the plates slip past each other. The energy is released, resulting in an earthquake that rattles the crust. When an earthquake happens in the ocean, the movement on the ocean floor displaces the water above it. Waves rush outward in the form of a tsunami. Eighty percent of tsunamis follow earthquakes. Rarer causes include volcanoes, landslides, and meteorites.

Tsunamis are dangerous because they happen so fast. People often don't have time to escape the waves. Over the years, people have built many cities along coastlines. Large **populations** are at risk when a tsunami hits. Moving water is heavy and powerful. And the danger does not end when the waves settle down. People who survive can have trouble getting food, shelter, and medical help.

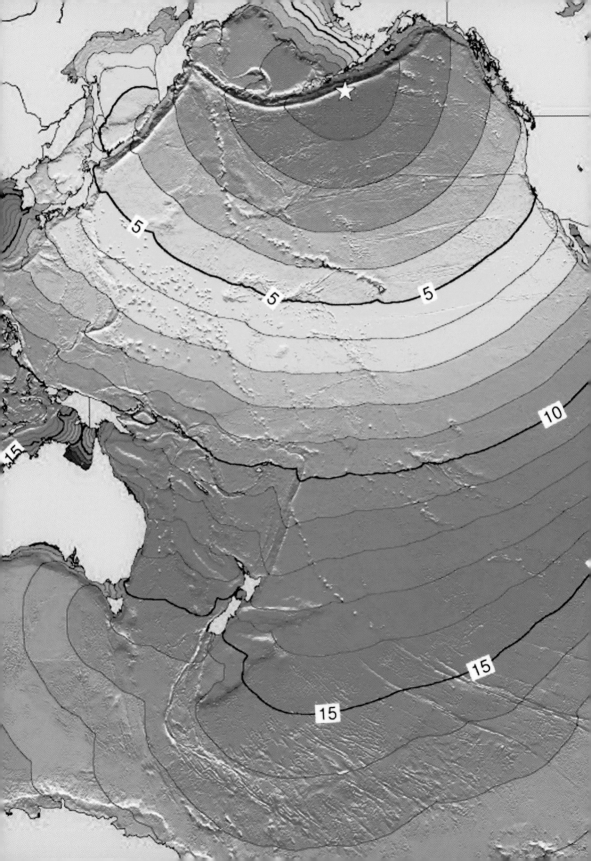

CHAPTER 3

TSUNAMI DETECTION

On April 1, 1946, a huge earthquake caused a tsunami that struck Alaska. Waves moved across the ocean to Hawaii, Asia, and the US West Coast. The tsunami killed 159 people.

After this disastrous event, the US government set up the Pacific Tsunami Warning Center, which is based in Hawaii.

This map of the 1946 tsunami shows how many hours it took the waves to reach each line.

Scientists there send warnings to Hawaii and island nations in the Pacific Ocean and the Caribbean Sea. The Indian Ocean Tsunami Warning System alerts nations that are in and around the Indian Ocean.

The National Tsunami Warning Center sends warnings to US coastal states, Puerto Rico, the Virgin Islands, and the Canadian coastal provinces. For earthquakes along the US coast, scientists can usually send out warnings within five minutes of the quake being detected. Worldwide, the time is approximately 10 minutes. Scientists are working to bring these times down.

Workers at the Pacific Tsunami Warning Center track a tsunami after detecting an earthquake.

Seismographs are instruments that record where and when earthquakes strike. Scientists use this information to alert people that an underwater earthquake might cause a tsunami. Sea level **gauges** measure tide levels.

Tsunami warning instruments are placed in the ocean to provide additional warning of approaching waves.

Scientists warn people if a tsunami is on the way to a shoreline.

Deep-ocean assessment and reporting of tsunamis (DART) stations are set up on the ocean floor. They collect data. Scientists use this information to help predict where a tsunami might hit. They can alert people in those areas.

A tsunami watch means an earthquake has hit the ocean floor. There is a chance a tsunami may strike. A tsunami warning means a tsunami is very likely. It means people must get to safety right away.

NOAA

The National Oceanic and Atmospheric Administration (NOAA) is an agency of the US government. Its scientists study the ocean and the atmosphere. They give people information so they can stay safe. They also help find ways to conserve ocean life and coastal land. The DART program is a part of NOAA.

DEEP-OCEAN ASSESSMENT AND REPORTING OF TSUNAMIS (DART)

In the DART system, sensors are placed on the ocean floor. When a tsunami wave reaches them, the sensors take measurements of the water pressure. They send this data to **buoys** on the surface, and the buoys pass the information to satellites. The satellites then beam the data down to scientists at warning centers. Scientists use the data to improve their computer models of where tsunamis start and where they will go.

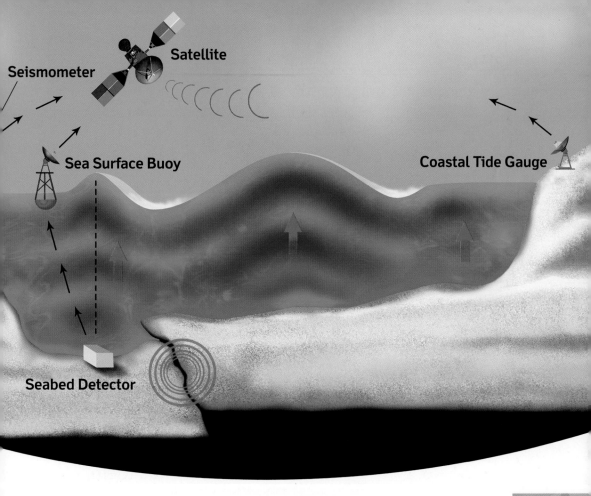

Seismometer

Satellite

Sea Surface Buoy

Coastal Tide Gauge

Seabed Detector

The DART system combines several technologies to collect data and improve tsunami computer models.

If the model shows that a tsunami is likely to be dangerous, the center sends out a warning to people in the affected area.

TSUNAMI HAZARD ZONE

ECO
SPIRITS
ecospirits.ch

IN CASE OF A
TSUNAMI ALERT
GO TO HIGH GROUND
OR ASSEMBLY AREA

CD
CIVIL
DEFENCE

FAR NORTH DISTRICT COUNCIL
EMERGENCY MANAGEMENT

Far North
District Council

CHAPTER 4

TSUNAMI SAFETY

In recent years, deadly tsunamis have struck Indonesia, Chile, Japan, and Samoa. Leaders in high-risk areas now help people learn about the warning signs of tsunamis. They teach people to get away from the ocean if the water pulls back. They make plans so people know where to go if a wave is coming.

Warning signs let people know about local tsunami risks.

In Japan, workers have built large walls to help protect parts of the coastline from tsunamis.

They remind people to stay away from the coast for several hours, because tsunamis include a series of waves.

Specially designed buildings in high-risk areas keep people safer if a tsunami hits. Engineers are finding ways to make buildings stronger. If there isn't time to **evacuate**, people can move to the top of a building. Japan is in a high-risk area for earthquakes and tsunamis.

TSUNAMI TYPES

There are different classifications of tsunamis. Local tsunamis wash over coasts within 62 miles (100 km) of the earthquake that caused them. They take an hour or less to hit. Regional tsunamis result from earthquakes between 62 miles (100 km) and 620 miles (1,000 km) away. These take from one to three hours to arrive. Ocean-wide tsunamis can start more than 620 miles (1,000 km) from the shoreline. It takes three or more hours for them to hit. The more time before a tsunami hits, the better the chance there is of sending out warnings so people can get to safety.

Engineers there make buildings that absorb shock. During an earthquake or tsunami, these buildings can shift around without breaking.

Scientists still cannot predict when and where a tsunami will hit. But in the past hundred years, they have learned a lot about how tsunamis happen. Advanced technology has allowed them to track these deadly waves. Scientists continue working to find better ways to detect tsunamis and save more lives.

TSUNAMI SAFETY CHECKLIST

- Make a tsunami evacuation plan with your family to figure out the safest place to go if a tsunami strikes.

- If a tsunami watch is announced, listen to a radio or watch television to get important updates.

- If a tsunami warning is announced or if you feel an earthquake near the ocean, immediately get to a safer place on higher ground.

- Never go down to the beach to watch a tsunami. Stay as far away from the beach as possible. Remember that tsunamis have more than one wave. The shore can remain dangerous for hours.

- If you notice an unusual amount of water receding, this is one sign of a tsunami. Move away from the beach right away.

- Look for anyone who might need help getting off the beach, such as infants, elderly people, or people with limited mobility, and help them evacuate to safety.

- Return home only after officials declare your area safe.

FOCUS ON
DETECTING TSUNAMIS

Write your answers on a separate piece of paper.

1. Summarize Chapter 2 of this book.

2. Do you think sending out a tsunami watch is a good idea? Or should scientists only send out tsunami warnings when a tsunami is very likely to occur? Why?

3. Why do many tsunamis happen in Japan?

   A. Earthquakes are common there.
   B. The winds are faster there.
   C. More meteorites fall there.

4. Which tsunami warning center would tell Californians that a tsunami was going to hit their state?

   A. the Pacific Tsunami Warning Center
   B. the National Tsunami Warning Center
   C. the Indian Ocean Tsunami Warning System

Answer key on page 32.

GLOSSARY

buoys
Floating objects anchored in the sea.

crest
The top of an individual wave.

displaces
Moves something out of position.

evacuate
To leave an area of danger.

gauges
Instruments for measuring.

marine biologist
A scientist who studies sea life.

plates
Sections of Earth's crust.

populations
The numbers of people living in particular areas.

seismographs
Instruments that measure and record the shaking of the ground.

TO LEARN MORE

BOOKS

Koontz, Robin. *The Science of a Tsunami.* Ann Arbor, MI: Cherry Lake, 2016.

Spilsbury, Richard, and Louise Spilsbury. *Sweeping Tsunamis.* Chicago: Heinemann Library, 2011.

Ventura, Marne. *Japan Earthquake and Tsunami Survival Stories.* Mankato, MN: The Child's World, 2016.

NOTE TO EDUCATORS

Visit **www.focusreaders.com** to find lesson plans, activities, links, and other resources related to this title.

INDEX

1946 Alaska earthquake, 17
2004 Indian Ocean tsunami, 5–9

DART system, 20–21, 22–23

earthquakes, 8, 13–15, 17–19, 21, 27, 28, 29
engineers, 26, 28

Indian Ocean Tsunami Warning System, 18

National Tsunami Warning Center, 18
NOAA, 21

Pacific Tsunami Warning Center, 17

safety, 21, 25–29
scientists, 9, 18–20, 21, 22, 28

Thailand, 5, 9
types of tsunamis, 27

waves, 7, 8, 9, 11–13, 15, 17, 22, 25, 26, 28

Answer Key: 1. Answers will vary; **2.** Answers will vary; **3.** A; **4.** B